I0210940

AUGUST 24, 1957

poems by

Robert Cooperman

Finishing Line Press
Georgetown, Kentucky

AUGUST 24, 1957

Copyright © 2025 by Robert Cooperman
ISBN 979-8-88838-938-6 First Edition
All rights reserved under International and Pan-American Copyright Conventions.
No part of this book may be reproduced in any manner whatsoever without written
permission from the publisher, except in the case of brief quotations embodied in
critical articles and reviews.

ACKNOWLEDGMENTS

Thanks to the following, where the poems listed below were published or are
forthcoming:

Bindweed: '"A Visit to My Primary Care Physician"
Blue Collar Review: "Blood"
Iconoclast: "My Right Hand"

Publisher: Leah Huete de Maines
Editor: Christen Kincaid
Cover Art: Gene McCormick
Author Photo: Beth Cooperman
Cover Design: Elizabeth Maines McCleavy

Order online: www.finishinglinepress.com
also available on amazon.com

Author inquiries and mail orders:
Finishing Line Press
PO Box 1626
Georgetown, Kentucky 40324
USA

Contents

For Michael and Steve,
Sorry About All the Trouble I Caused

And as ever and forever, for Beth,
Who Saved Me in More Ways Than One

Shattered Glass

Last night, a Wizard of Oz wind
knocked down our patio chairs,
the top-heavy umbrella dragging
the table over, shattering the glass,
shards splattering, gales howling
too hard for us to gather the slivers.

Suddenly, I was eleven again, running
into the apartment house vestibule,
one hand on the wood frame,
the other shoving the glass
that gave from a hairline crack, blood
exploding, the odds I'd live not great.

But I did, so now I blink, blink again,
and with Beth, grab the chairs
and shove them into the shed,
and inspect the damage.

"I'll clean it up tomorrow,"
I shudder, glad, in the growing dark,
she can't see memories slapping my face:
flinching at the sight of all that glass.

Some Things

Some things you don't forget.
Alas, I fail to recall the names
of acquaintances, from time
to mortifying time.
Likewise, I neglect to take my meds,
so use the mnemonic of turning the bottles
upside down after I pop a capsule,
right-side up, a few hours later.

What I mean is that childhood accident
that almost made me a legend
among my friends, for dying young,
and an object lesson for their parents
to bludgeon their kids with, loudly:
"Don't run into glass doors!"

For decades, I hadn't thought
of that August morning that started golden,
and ended up a geyser of me.
But for the past few years, I'll brush
the raised scar on my wrist, or see
a shattered bottle, or TV violence,
or almost anything,

and I'm eleven again, blood a burst main,
my buddies frozen, my mother screaming
to haul me to the doctor around the block,
his wife-receptionist loudly trying to bar me
from spilling blood on the waiting room carpet,
until Dr. Levine shoved her aside and fulfilled
his Hippocratic oath of saving my life.

"Why has that memory returned now?"
I keep asking myself. Maybe a reminder
I've used up most of the years
Time wants me to pay back.

Even As

Even as my mother was screaming,
"You will not die, damnit!" yanking me
along to Dr. Levine's office down the block,
blood pumping from my wrist, elbow
and upper arm, I kept thinking,

"It's just blood, not a compound fracture."

We burst through his front door,
met by his wife-receptionist-witch,
who tried to push me back into the street.

"He'll ruin my carpet!" she screeched:
Dr. Levine shoved her aside,
yanked me onto the exam table,
and ordered her to hand him instruments,
while he tourniqueted my arm
and jammed the numbing syringe
into the raw hamburger of the open wound.
I shrieked: the needle a jabbing agony
and finally, it hit me that yes,

I might die, though he patted my arm,
murmured as if to a lightning-frightened colt,
tied arteries, refolded the huge flap of skin
back over my wrist, then reached
for the surgical thread—humming
like Mom darning socks—
while she paced the waiting room,
sobbed, demanded to know how I was,
then to use the phone, to call my dad.

Woozy, I shuddered to think of all that blood
and our apartment house's shattered-glass
vestibule door, and how, on my quarter-
a-week-allowance, would I ever
pay for all the damage I'd done.

Cab Ride to Brookdale Hospital

After the doctor had stitched
and swaddled my ripped-up right arm
in mummy bandages, and shot me
full of enough painkillers
to turn my legs to Jell-o,
my brains even more jiggly,

he advised my mother
to take me by taxi to the hospital,
where they'd re-operate on his patchwork.

"The ambulance will gouge you
like a melon baller," he shook his head,
and told his receptionist-nurse-pain-
in-the-ass-wife to call a cab for us.

While my mother quietly cried
as we rode, I drug-mumbled
reassurances to her and myself:

"It's not as bad as a broken arm, Mom."

Waking Up My First Morning at Brookdale Hospital

Something was weighing me down.
Prying open my eyes
from my painkiller haze, I saw
the cast, heavy as a battleship's anchor.

When I tried to rise—my bladder
beating like Hi-Ho Silver!—
a nurse gentled me back down,
handed me a bedpan.
I may have been eleven,
but I figured it out.

Then it came at me
like a snarling dog: the memory
of that shattering glass-door
I idiot-ran-into,
as if trying to outrun
St. Rose of Lima High School
hitters and rocks.

A scream started to rise,
the nurse shushing me,
wiping my swamp-wet forehead,
until my parents peered in,
my dad tussling my hair,
my mom kissing me,
through my quieting breaths.

I wasn't fooled by his,
"Hey Pal," smile:
her cheery lipstick,

that was, after all, almost
as red as my blood
that had spasmed
over everything.

The Children's Ward

My second night after surgery,
they rolled in another kid: his face
the sick green of a tornado sky.

A priest gave him, what even I,
a Jewish kid of eleven, knew
were the last rites for Catholics
who might not make it.

After the priest left, they rolled
the kid out for emergency surgery.
I willed myself asleep, too afraid
I'd see an orderly strip the bed
the kid was never going to need.

But in the morning, I heard
his mother murmuring,

"Thank God, thank God,"
clicking her rosary beads I knew
from a Cagney movie,
didn't always work.

But this time, I thought
maybe I should convert,
except hadn't Elohim made sure
Dr. Levine lived just
around the block,

His mysterious-as-always
way of protecting a kid
stupid enough
to run through a glass door?

The Battle of the Children's Ward

After my new best friend Tony was discharged,
I was alone, until his bed was polluted by Myron,
a mouthy appendix-removed brat who bragged
his father was a *macher* who'd have my family killed
when I wouldn't let Myron steal the coins
my dad had given me for a comic book.

When I fumbled over food with the one hand
not manacled inside the cast, Myron would point,
"Whatsa matter, Spazz, having trouble?"

And while he watched TV loud enough
to drown out the Coney Island roller coaster,
I ripped the cord from the outlet,
and when he went for me, I belted him
with my cast; lucky I didn't rip any stitches.

His father, dressed like a vice-principal,
suddenly appeared, accusing, "Juvenile
delinquent; I'll have you arrested!"

"Like hell you will!" my dad, also arriving,
shouted back. "Your *vantz* got what was coming,"
Dad ready to throw jabs at the guy's sloppy belly,
while Myron blushed, almost blubbered
when his father backed down, and I silently cheered
for blood to be spilled, that, this time,

didn't fountain out of me.

The Smuggled Pastrami Sandwich

Brookdale Hospital frowned on
outside food for us patients.
Or was that inmates?
The food, classic hospital swill:
revolting oatmeal, mac and cheese
resembling orange worms,
ubiquitous Jell-o shimmying
like toxic swamp ooze.
If you were lucky, cold cereal,
burnt scrambled eggs.

Once, we got steak for dinner;
my right arm in a cast, I couldn't
cut what passed for meat: more like steel
that could withstand anything
less lethal than a battleax.

So one afternoon, my darling Aunt Roz
smuggled in a pastrami on rye
from Aaron's Deli. She sat on my bed
and fed me slices juicier than the jowls
of feasting Vikings. And did I mention
the French fries, the sour pickle?

Despite the weight of that cast,
the maddening sting of all the stitches—
over sixty when they stopped counting—
plus the memory of shattered glass and blood,
I felt light as Pepsi bubbles.

Later, they served gulag dinner-slop.

"Eat up," the nurse cajoled, trying
to shovel the glop into my mouth.
"It's good for you. And so delicious!"

The Little Book of Horses

The one day they let friends visit me,
Ricky, the oldest kid in our building,
so least likely to be infected by a dread
hospital disease, the kid we all hero worshipped
for his moves on the playground b-ball court,
and the moves he made on our building's teenage girls—
handed me a quarto-sized book and shrugged.

Shakespeare? Whom I wouldn't have understood,
at eleven, even with tutorials from Harold Bloom.
Nah, *The Little Book of Horses*: instant love:
photos and descriptions of each breed: a bible
of my totem animal, always drawing horses' heads
in textbook margins and on looseleaf pages.

I was mesmerized by the Arabian, hot blooded
as the desert; its cousins, the Turk and Barb;
the thoroughbred; Appaloosa; palomino; quarter horse.
But I studied every entry as a sacred text,
astounded by the schlong—no other word for
the baseball-bat-length-phallus—on the Shire,
the world's biggest horse.

Even after my wounds healed, I spent hours
staring at the photos, reading the descriptions.
Years later, when I left Brooklyn
for grad school in Denver, that book got lost.

A year later, visiting my mom, with Beth,
I ran into Ricky; after our, "Yo, how you doin'?"
I reminded him how much I'd appreciated
that little book in the hospital.

"I stole it," he laughed, "thinking
it was something, y'know, more interesting,"
he winked, waved goodbye, gone.

Blood

When I returned from my ten-days
of being held hostage at Brookdale Hospital—
to a kid of eleven, longer than Odysseus's
years of wandering—the glass hadn't
been replaced in our building's door
I'd burst through, just a plywood covering.

And the blood that had pumped out of me
as I ran, terrified, screaming for my mother's
miracle of instant healing, still hadn't
been mopped up from the foyer floor,
the stairs, our second floor corridor,
and ended only at our apartment's front door.

It took another week of my parents'
disgusted complaints and threats to withhold
sacred rent, to get the management to get
the super to get a glazier in, and to clean up
the mess, before he resumed his other duty
as the building's unofficial bookmaker.

But to me, the blood was my red badge
of, if not courage exactly, then fame:
the kid who'd survived the bloodbath
that made Al Capone's tommy gun antics
look like a blood blister or mosquito bite;

the kid who walked around with a cast
heavy as the barbells another kid
in the building pumped religiously
as if laying *tefillin* for prayers.

I could almost convince myself
that my plaster cast, signed by friends
and family, made me a hero returned
from war, unlike the one, a decade later
two of my friends never came home from.

What the Neighbors Thought of Me

To the other kids,
for a week or so,
I was the miracle
whose arm had been raked
as if by a tiger shark,
who'd survived the shattered
glass door, blood a splatter-
painting all over the foyer,
the super too lazy
or freaked to mop up.

But soon I was just Bobby,
the kid who'd rather read
than play punchball, stickball,
touch football, or anything;
and now had no choice.

The adults? Some thought
I was a quiet kid
who'd gotten a deal rawer
than spoiled hamburger meat,
smiling at me when I'd read
under the front yard tree.

To others, I was that crazy
Cooperman kid, hurtling
through that glass door,
as if on a dare; conveniently,
forgetting their own kids ran up,
one hand on the wood panel,
the other shoving the glass,
hurrying to get to their apartments,

But after a while, no one cared,
too busy with their own lives.
And, in truth, even to me,
it was old news.

Removing the Cast

I feared I'd have to wear
that anvil-heavy cast forever,
forever use the side of a fork
to saw one-handed at food.

In muttering frustration,
I'd grab the meat with my good
left hand and bite off a chunk,
my kid brother snorting,
my parents demanding why
hadn't I waited for one of them
to cut the food into pieces
small enough for an infant.

That cast was punishment
for being stupid enough to shatter
our apartment house vestibule's
glass door: like Sisyphus,
splattered each time he grunted
that boulder almost to the top
of that hill in Tartarus.

But a month later, the surgeon
worked a metal jaw under the cast
while I slammed shut my eyes,
afraid that monster would take off
my arm, but a snip, a crunch,
and he peeled back the cast.
The arm? It could've floated,
or held the warm hand of Lenore Levy
whom I couldn't help stealing glances at,
in seventh grade,

though I knew the sight of that
still oozing scar would make her
run for her life.

Practicing Scales on a Neighbor's Piano

At eleven, I had no illusion
I could be a second Van Cliburn.
It was all about unloosening the fingers

on my right hand, the hand that had plunged
through the hairline fractured glass
of our apartment house's front door,

the hand that was stiff as a mounted
raven's talons, after the bandages
had come off, and the wound no longer oozed

like a puke-green oil slick.
Our neighbor, Mrs. Cohen, taught music
and when the doctor declared I needed

to start using my right hand again,
or forever forget I had one,
Mrs. Cohen had me practicing scales,

my fingers clumsy as Frankenstein's monster,
staggering from a torch-and-pitchfork mob.
I never attained basic competence,

let alone the spider dexterity
of a Little Richard or Jerry Lee Lewis.
The only reason I kept returning?

Her daughter, Alice, two years older,
and maybe she'd be impressed, if
I'd played Beethoven's "Fur Elise"

like the Maestro. So, I fumbled along.

The Rubber Ball

After I gave up playing piano scales,
to try to unloosen the rusty hinges
of my devastated right hand,

my doctor gave me a rubber ball,
a Spalding, the brand we played
punchball and stickball with.

Except, these days, I could only watch.
"Squeeze this," Dr. Levine urged.
"Squeeze and release, squeeze and release."

A lot easier than trying to crab-scramble
my fingers along a piano's keyboard,
especially since Mrs. Cohen's daughter—

beautiful Alice, unapproachable Alice,
two years-older-than-me Alice—was swooning
over the doo-wop rocks outside Rudy's candy store

whenever I showed up at her mother's apartment,
to play scales like a drunken tarantula, and to stammer
something I thought brilliant, flirtatious.

So the Spalding it was, until I could hold
a pen or pencil with my right hand and scrawl
something not entirely illegible, though I had the sense

not to try to Palmer Method love-poems to Alice,
who, if I'd been lucky, would've sneered
and tossed the embarrassing verses into the trash,

instead of showing them to her hitter-hoodlum
boyfriend, who'd have read them aloud
for the whole school yard to snicker at.

The Door: August-November, 1957

To make sure no one else
shattered the vestibule glass-door,
and to further ensure no one else
could sue, the super drilled a lock
on the front door.

So even if your bladder was bursting,
or Tommy Lockhart was breathing
hell and murder down your back,
you had to stop and find the key.

The melodramatist in me wants
to say I shuddered, in troubled,
blood-drenched memory, each time
I fumbled the key into the lock.
In truth? I hardly thought about it.

What I did think about,
what everyone thought about:
the Sputnik satellite,
buzzard-circling, spying, taunting:
Khrushchev's godless commies
beating us into space,
owning the stars, owning us.

By comparison, my scarred wrist,
my right hand without much feeling
or mobility? Far less important
than nuclear annihilation;
and even worse, not even close
to our beloved Dodgers
deserting Brooklyn for L.A.

The Sling

After I woke from surgery,
a cast heavy as a Civil War fieldpiece,

the nurse showed me how to attach the sling;
otherwise, the arm would've dangled

from the cast's almost dead weight,
like a frigate's cracked four pounders.

A month later, the wound healed,
my muscle memory so used to the sling,

I held my forearm as if it was still supported,
like a dog offering that appendage, to "shake."

That was a lifetime ago, but sometimes,
I catch myself wearing that invisible sling:

the arm resting, nonchalant, casual
as a tattered flannel shirt I just couldn't

bring myself to toss away: no matter
that I can still hear shattering glass.

My Right Hand

After my shattering encounter
with our building's glass front door,
my right hand was frozen at age eleven,
the feeling gone: the surgeon explaining
about severed nerves never growing back.

I took class notes with my left hand,
drove to the bucket, and shot—badly—lefty
in recess b-ball games, after
a purgatory of watching, healing;

and used my left hand to button up
my school shirts, getting the cuffs
lined up: the finger-fumbling part
I wanted no one else to see, and sneer,

"Hey, man, what a spazz!"

Still, I was careful, so no one
seemed to notice the toad-huge bump
on my right wrist, or that sometimes
the fingers were stiff and creaky
as rusted nails and screws,

until I finally figured out
no one was really all that interested.

Walking Home from Ditmas Junior High School

My right hand in a sling,
I'd walk to and from school
with friends: safety in numbers,
especially on the perilous journey home:
hitters swaggering out of
nearby St. Rose Catholic School,
demanding payment for safe passage.

One Friday afternoon, staying late
for the creative writing club,
I had to walk alone.
On that long, lonely stretch
of Prospect Parkway, three rocks
slouching against a tree,
waiting for a little kid
to pummel and rob.

But something scratched
under my coward skin,
and instead of blubbering coins
into their grimy palms,
I ripped off the bandage
and shoved my green, oozing wrist
into the lead wolf's face.

Instead of puking, he held my hand,
gently as the nurses had, and stared.

"Wow, man, did you try
to off yourself? That'd be a mortal
sin, but I can sorta dig it,
if your old man ain't no better'n mine.
So listen, man, you ever need help,
you know where we hang."

Then, like wolves, they were gone.

One Good Thing

One good thing
about my blood-splattered
collision with the glass door
to our apartment house's vestibule:

I never had to play,
"Johnny on the Pony," again:
my right wrist too weak
to bear the thunderous weight
of rival teams trying to break
my leaned-over hold on the kid
in front of me, enemy kids—
flying onto our backs like an evil
Roy Rogers mounting a cringing
Trigger on the run—demanding,

"Buck, buck, how many fingers are up?"

If we didn't guess right,
we'd have to bend and await
the rubber ball hurled
at our backsides, by a kid
most likely beaten every night
by his drunken old man, so anyone
he could take out that rage and pain on,
well, rough darts, as we used to say,
meaning, "Too freakin' bad."

Pardoned, I got to read,
looked up every now and then,
to see whose heinie
was getting walloped: grateful
my right hand was shriveled,
less feeling than Captain Hook's hook.

Before and After

Before I slashed through that glass door,
I loved playing handball,
so satisfying to smack a kill shot,
my palm ringing with the blood-
knowledge I'd won the point.
Either hand, I was pretty good.

But after that accident, that fountain
of blood, the hospital, the squeezing
of a rubber ball, the spastic playing of scales
to get some mobility back into my fingers—
the one time I swung righty, pain exploded
from my palm up to my shoulder:
alas, the end of my handball career,

though I still loved watching my dad
play at the Brighton Beach courts:
younger guys sucking wind
in their hubris at deigning to play
"an old man," they could take, easy,

even as I lamented I could never
be that master of strategy again,
that deliverer of unreturnable shots,
with an all-powerful right hand.

The Settlement

Despite confessing to my parents
it was my stupidity: to run through
that glass door in our apartment house's foyer,
my parents sued, my father lecturing:

"The glass had a crack everyone could see,
and people shoved through that door
since before I can remember."

The year before, I'd ordered what I thought
were real Civil War stamps, from the back
of a comic book: when they arrived: "Replicas."
Only right I shouldn't pay for false advertising.

But when the letters landed like the splayed
talons of buzzards, threatening lawsuits, prison,
I trembled them to my dad, who dictated,
"Dear Sirs, I am ten-years-old. Screw you."
End of my legal problems.

But five years after I tore up my wrist,
my parents, lawyer, and I were summoned
for depositions. I was grilled as if I'd murdered
the whole Borough of Brooklyn.

The resulting settlement, not nearly enough
for my folks to retire on, for Dad to play
pinochle and the ponies, Mom to employ
a cleaning lady, enjoy mahjong and martinis,

and for Jeff and me to attend Harvard,
as if they'd take two dolts like us.
Still, that settlement got me a summer
in England, though I'd tried to share

the payout, putting my parents through
tzuris enough for two or three lifetimes.

One Time: Greenwich Village, 1971

One time, when I was rolling joints
at a New Year's Eve party—
fumbling with my savaged right hand,
the Dead blasting from the stereo,
friends dancing, munching, ambling over
to make conversation—this one guy,
with a skull and crossbones belt buckle,
a crimson silk pirate shirt,
and black leather pants, snickered,

"Sort of spastic, ain't-cha?"
and grabbed my wrist to see the scars,
the stopped-growing-at-eleven-fingers,
the middle finger I couldn't straighten
into a "fuck you, asshole," sign,
if I'd beaten it with a hammer.

Some people, when they caught a glimpse,
before I quickly hid my wrist, stared;
some looked away fast, afraid
they'd be turned to stone.
One woman traced the raised ridges
as if studying a tarot card.

"Man," this guy shrugged,
"you're one careless twit,"
before I yanked my wrist away
and told him to screw off.

Now, I'd wonder: was he a soulless
Republican hedge-fund manager
badly disguised as a hippie?

Back then, he was just a putz.

A Visit to My Primary Care Physician

The examination over,
the two of us *kveling* about the Nuggets,
I started to put on my shirt,
when Dr. Abrams noticed
the raised scar on my right wrist.

"Why didn't you tell me about this cyst?
he stared at the bump. "We should get it biopsied."

"It's scar tissue, from when I went through
the glass door in my parents' building's vestibule."

"But why's it raised?" he demanded.

"The surgeon told me he had to tie off
the tendons and blood vessels inside the wrist,
with some sort of surgical thread."

"Really?" he was fascinated, his days mostly
spent warning patients about blood pressure,
diabetes, lipids, and cholesterol.

"That's what he told me," I shrugged.
"But I was eleven, and would've believed
anything from the guy who'd just saved my life."

Another doctor, years ago, had assured me,

"We can do plastic surgery on that now,
so the wrist will look like new."

I told him it was sort of an old friend,
or at the least a traveling companion
I couldn't abandon by the side of the road.

Dispensations

I used to think that because I'd already
almost died in that childhood collision

with the hairline fractured glass door,
I'd earned a dispensation—like a hall pass—

from further injury or illness, until, say,
the age of 100 or so, when, I'd pass,

gentle and painless as a blown-out
Chanukah candle into whatever next life

or nothing there was.
Alas, one bit of stupidity doesn't cancel out

all the crap life gleefully flings.
But I've decided not to think of the cancer,

coronary, or more exotic closers,
that will sooner than later come for me.

Or rather, I don't think of those killers
too often, grateful for Beth, my brother,

friends, the family that's left.
Though every now and then, I glance

at my savaged wrist, and for a second or two,
I'm going through that glass door again:

my own little death, and not the delightful one.

Robert Cooperman was born and bred in Brooklyn, New York, where the action of August 24, 1957 takes place one fateful morning. Luckily, Cooperman survived his little encounter with a glass vestibule door that had a hairline fracture in it and eventually went on to leave New York for Denver and grad school. Cooperman has taught at the University of Georgia, Bowling Green State University, and the University of Baltimore. His poetry has appeared in over twenty full-length collections and ten chapbooks, *August 24, 1957*, being the latest one. *In the Colorado Gold Fever Mountains* won the Colorado Book Award for Poetry in 2000. *Draft Board Blues* was named One of the Ten Best Books by a Colorado Author for 2017, by *Westword Magazine*. Cooperman lives in Denver with his wife Beth.

www.ingramcontent.com/pod-product-compliance
Lightning Source LLC
Chambersburg PA
CBHW022101080426
42734CB00009B/1444